Comprehension

Pupil Book **Year 3**

Rachel Axten-Higgs

Features of this book

- Clear explanations and worked examples for each comprehension topic from the KS2 National Curriculum.

- Questions split into three sections that become progressively more challenging:

  Warm up

  Test yourself

  Challenge yourself

- 'How did you do?' checks at the end of each topic for self-evaluation.

- Regular progress tests to assess pupils' understanding and recap on their learning.

- Answers to every question in a pull-out section at the centre of the book.

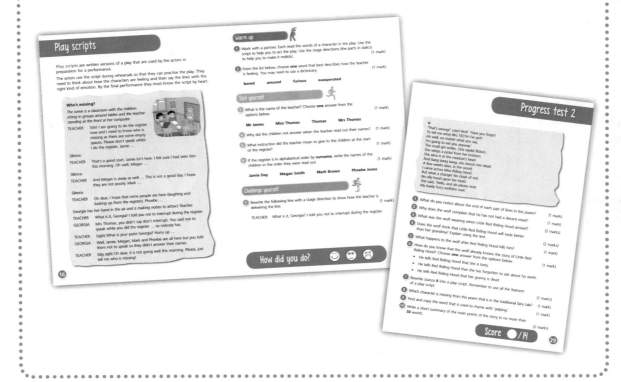

Contents

Fairy tales

A **fairy tale** is a short story that usually features magic and fantasy characters, such as talking animals or fairies.

The typical structure of a fairy tale is that a bad character is defeated, changed or made good, and the good characters live happily ever after.

The Frog Prince

Once upon a time there lived a very spoilt princess. One day she took her golden ball into the woods. As she walked she threw the ball up into the air, and, on the third throw, the ball rolled into a deep well. She shouted and kicked the well but with no luck. She was just about to kick the well again when a frog plopped out from it.

'Yuck,' said the princess.

'What are you making such a noise and fuss about?' asked the frog.

The princess was speechless; a talking frog! It didn't take long for her to recover and she told the frog about her lost ball and how she wanted it back. The frog jumped in and retrieved it. The princess went to snatch it from him, but the frog told her to ask for it nicely; reluctantly she did. Before the frog gave the ball to the princess he told her that, in return, he wanted to live with her in the palace, eat from her plate and sleep on her pillow. The princess was not happy but wanted her ball back, so she agreed (thinking that a promise to a frog wouldn't matter). She went back to the palace with her ball.

That evening, when the family sat down to eat, they heard a voice – it was the frog asking for the princess. She had to explain to her parents what had happened, and they told her that she had to keep her promise. So, the frog sat next to her at the table (she did not eat a thing). He slept on the bed with her (she did not sleep a wink). This happened again on the second day.

By the third day, the princess was so hungry she ate from her plate. She was so tired, she slept through the night. On the morning of the fourth day she woke up and looked for the frog. He was not there. Standing at the foot of her bed, however, was a handsome prince.

'Who are you?' she screamed.

'I was the frog who rescued your golden ball. I was bewitched by a fairy who told me I was rude and spoilt. She said the spell could only be broken by someone equally rude and spoilt having to be nice to me … so, here I am!'

1. Name **two** other fairy tales that you have read. (1 mark)

2. Name **three** types of characters that are often found in fairy tales, such as fairies. (1 mark)

3. Write down **three** key features of fairy tales. (1 mark)

Test yourself

4. Who told the princess she had to keep her promise? Choose **one** answer from the options below. (1 mark)

   the frog   **herself**   **her parents**   **the fairy**

5. Why was the princess speechless when she met the frog? (1 mark)

6. Why do you think the princess did not eat anything on the first and second days? (2 marks)

7. What do you think the prince's experience taught him about how to treat people? (1 mark)

Challenge yourself

8. Write down **two** magical features of the story. (2 marks)

9. The princess could be described as the bad and the good character in the story. What evidence is there that she was bad? (2 marks)

How did you do?

The language of fairy tales

You probably know the **language of fairy tales** quite well. They often have well-known phrases, such as:

Once upon a time …

They all lived happily ever after.

Fairy tales are for children and their language reflects this. Fairy tales often use repetitive language.

Cinderella

Once upon a time, a grand invitation went out explaining that the Prince was holding a ball for all the young ladies in the land so that he could choose one to marry. The Ugly Sisters were very excited and bought new dresses for the occasion. They made Cinderella help them get ready for days in advance.

On the evening of the ball, the Ugly Sisters left and Cinderella sat down on the kitchen step and cried; she had nothing to wear and no way of getting to the ball. Suddenly, there was a swirl of colours and an old lady was standing in front of Cinderella.

'You shall go to the ball, Cinderella!' she said.

With that, the Fairy Godmother turned a pumpkin into a golden coach, then turned her wand on Cinderella. Suddenly, Cinderella was wearing an amazing ball gown, sparkling tiara and beautiful glass slippers. She would go to the ball!

'Have fun, but leave before midnight, as that is when the magic will wear off and you'll be back in your old clothes!' the Fairy Godmother said.

When Cinderella arrived at the ball she was a dazzling beauty whom nobody recognised. The Prince hurried to dance with her; the Ugly Sisters were furious! Cinderella was enjoying herself so much that she forgot the Fairy Godmother's warning. The clock began to strike midnight. She turned from the Prince, and ran down the stairs to her coach, accidently dropping one of her glass slippers on the way.

The next day, the Prince and his servants went from house to house looking for the girl whose foot would fit the slipper. When they arrived at Cinderella's house, the Ugly Sisters were still in a towering rage. They tried the slipper on first; it didn't fit. Cinderella asked to try it; the sisters laughed, but the shoe fitted her perfectly. The Prince looked into Cinderella's face and saw the beautiful eyes from the night before. He married her the very next day and they lived happily ever after.

1. Write down the traditional opening and ending that are used in this story. (2 marks)

2. Who is the magical character in this story? How does the author describe this character? (2 marks)

3. Who was the 'dazzling beauty'? Choose **one** answer from the options below. (1 mark)

Ugly Sister   **Fairy Godmother**   **Cinderella**   **Prince**

4. Why were the Ugly Sisters 'in a towering rage' the morning after the ball? (2 marks)

5. Put the following events in the correct order, to show the story from start to finish. (2 marks)

- Cinderella arrived at the ball.
- The Fairy Godmother transformed Cinderella.
- Cinderella helped the Ugly Sisters get ready for the ball.
- Cinderella and the Prince got married.
- The clock struck midnight.

6. The author has used adjectives to provide extra description. Find and copy an adjective that is used to describe Cinderella at the ball. (1 mark)

7. The Ugly Sisters were not happy at the end of the story. Do you feel sorry for them? Explain your answer giving evidence from the text. (2 marks)

How did you do?

Themes in fairy tales

Fairy tales often involve princes and princesses who want to get married. Usually, as they are the good characters, their wishes come true and they are happily married by the end of the story! This is just one of a number of common **themes** that run through fairy tales. Others that you need to look out for include:

- good conquering evil
- characters seeking happiness
- heroic rescues.

The Princess and the Pea

Once upon a time there lived a prince who was very fed up. He wanted to get married. Everyone thought he should get married. The problem was that he would only marry a true princess. He had met many girls who *claimed* to be princesses, but they turned out not to be *true* princesses. The prince had given up hope and instead sat in the palace feeling miserable.

One night there was a terrible storm. Rain lashed down, thunder rumbled close by and lightning forks lit the sky around the palace. Everyone huddled together, close to the fire. Suddenly, the front door bell rang, cutting through the storm. The prince rushed to open the door.

Standing on the doorstep, dripping wet, was a princess…well, she said she was a princess but the prince would not be fooled so easily. She didn't look much like a princess in her dripping clothes and she was all alone, without a maid.

The queen decided to test the girl, so she instructed the maids to make up a bed in the second-best bedroom (not the best bedroom, as she might not be a princess). She told the maids to take all the bedding and the mattress from the bed and then placed one single pea in the middle of the bedframe. The maids then piled twenty-five mattresses and twenty-five soft quilts on top.

The girl was then left to sleep on the bed for the night. In the morning, the queen entered the bedroom and asked the girl how she had slept.

'I didn't sleep a wink all night long,' replied the girl. 'There was a great, hard lump in the middle of the bed – it was quite horrible.'

Everyone knew by this that the girl was a true princess. The prince was so happy that he married her the very next day and they lived happily ever after.

1 Write down **three** characters that are in this story that are often found in other fairy tales. (3 marks)

2 How is the ending, and what happens to the characters, similar to other fairy tales? (1 mark)

Test yourself

3 Why was the prince miserable at the start? Choose **one** answer from the options below. (1 mark)

- He was fed up with eating peas.
- He couldn't find a real princess.
- He hated princesses.

4 Why did the prince think that she was not a princess when he first saw her? (1 mark)

5 Find and copy the words the author has used to show that the rain was falling heavily. (1 mark)

Challenge yourself

6 In your own words, explain how everyone knew that the princess was 'a true princess' by the end of the story. (2 marks)

7 Why was it important to the queen and the prince that the girl was a 'real' princess? (2 marks)

How did you do?

Drawing inferences

An **inference** is a conclusion or a judgement based on evidence or reasoning.

In books, authors often tell you more than they say directly. They give clues or hints that help the reader to 'read between the lines'.

When you use these clues to give you a better understanding of the text, it is called **inferring**.

Extract from *Grimble* by Clement Freud

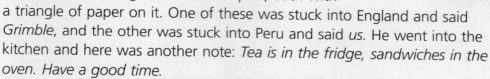

One Monday Grimble came back from school, opened the door and shouted, 'I am home.' No one shouted anything in answer. So he went round the house looking for messages because his parents always left messages. It was the one thing they were really good at.

On a table in the sitting room there was a globe. And stuck into the globe were two pins, each with a triangle of paper on it. One of these was stuck into England and said *Grimble*, and the other was stuck into Peru and said *us*. He went into the kitchen and here was another note: *Tea is in the fridge, sandwiches in the oven. Have a good time.*

In the bedroom was a note saying *You will do your homework, won't you? P.S. don't forget to say your prayers.*

In the bathroom a message *Teeth*.

He walked round the house thinking they've really been very good, and then he went to the back-door and saw a note: *Milkman. No milk for five days.*

He changed the note to *Not much milk for five days*, and sat down in the kitchen and started to think about things. Five days is a long time for anyone and an especially long time for a boy of ten who is never quite sure whether he might not be missing his birthday. It had been weeks since he last had a birthday. He got a piece of paper and worked out five days at twenty-four hours a day and made it over a hundred hours, actually a hundred and something hours. He decided to have a sandwich. He opened the oven door, found the oven absolutely full of sandwiches, and took one with corned beef and apricot jam in it.

1 Where had Grimble's parents gone? (1 mark)

2 What did Grimble think about the length of time his parents were going to be away for? How do you know? (2 marks)

Test yourself

3 What was the **one** thing that Grimble's parents were really good at? Choose **one** answer from the options below. (1 mark)

- reading him bedtime stories
- being good parents
- making sandwiches
- leaving messages

4 Why did the note that his parents had written for the milkman make Grimble think that they had not been so good after all? (1 mark)

5 How long are Grimble's parents planning to be away? How do you know? (2 marks)

Challenge yourself

6 Do you think Grimble's parents are being good parents? (2 marks)

7 What do you think the message 'Teeth' meant? (1 mark)

How did you do?

Justifying inferences

Sometimes you will be asked to **justify** your inferences. In order to do this, you will need to use evidence from the text (for example, what the author actually says) to explain how you came to your conclusion.

Shipwreck

It was early morning when we heard the church bells ringing. It wasn't Sunday so we knew there wasn't a church service. There was only one thing it could be. A shipwreck!

Pulling on his boots, Dad grabbed some toast and dashed out of the door. I wanted to follow but I knew Mum wouldn't let me go until I had finished my porridge.

By the time we got down to the shore, we could see the wreck, jammed on the rocks off Tinker's Point. Dozens of little fishing boats were heading towards it in the sea. I knew Dad's boat would be out there somewhere, but I couldn't see it.

Boats were wrecked on those rocks every year. I knew the ship would not sink for now. It would be stuck on the rocks until the tide washed it free later in the day. There was always plenty of time to rescue the crew.

The barrels and crates the ship was carrying were another matter. Once the men from the ship were safely ashore, anyone with a little boat would be back in the water again, fishing for crates of colourful silk, fancy tea sets or spices from far away.

Warm up

1. How do the villagers know that there has been a shipwreck?
   Choose **two** answers from the options below.

   (1 mark)

   - The rocks are dangerous.
   - The church bells are ringing.
   - Somebody is shouting it.
   - It is not Sunday.

2 What did the narrator have to finish before leaving the house?
Choose **one** answer from the options below. (1 mark)

breakfast   **lunch**   **dinner**   **a snack**

3 From this text you could make the following inference: **the narrator has seen ships wrecked on those rocks before**. Write down **two** pieces of evidence to justify this inference. (2 marks)

4 Why do you think the narrator's mother would not let her go before she had finished her porridge? (2 marks)

5 Why do you think that the narrator 'knew Dad's boat would be out there somewhere'? (2 marks)

6 How does the narrator know that the crew will be saved? (2 marks)

7 The little fishing boats were going out to rescue the crew first. How do you know this? (2 marks)

8 Re-read paragraph 4. What do you think will happen to the boat when the tide washes it free later in the day? Explain your answer using information in the text. (2 marks)

How did you do?

The Three Little Pigs

Once upon a time there were three little
pigs. They lived with their mother in a
small house. They had healthy appetites
and the more they ate, the more they
grew. The pigs grew bigger and bigger
and it seemed like the house grew

smaller and smaller, until finally their mother said they would have to move
out and find houses of their own. She was sad to see them go but was
pleased to have more space for herself again! She warned them to be careful
and stay away from the Big Bad Wolf who lived in the woods.

The three pigs set off along the path into the woods. The first pig was afraid
of the dark and wanted to build his house quickly before the evening came.
He saw a man selling straw and decided to buy some there and then and
build his house immediately. The other two pigs helped him to ensure it was
built quickly. They all stayed the night in the straw house, which was very
comfortable, if a little cold.

The next morning, the two little pigs waved goodbye to their brother and
continued along the winding path into the woods. The second little pig
decided that he would like to get a roof over his head quickly too but did
not want it to be as cold as the straw house of his brother. He saw a man
selling sticks and decided to buy some. He and his brother built a very sturdy
little house of sticks. The brothers stayed in the house and the third little pig
worked very hard drawing plans, phoning builders and suppliers ready to
make his house, for he had decided to make his house of bricks.

Finally, after two weeks, the house of bricks was ready for the third little pig
to move in. He was very comfortable there and even had a beautiful fireplace
to keep him warm.

Before long, the Big Bad Wolf, who had been away on holiday in a different
wood terrorising a girl dressed in a red cloak, came back to the woods. The
three little houses intrigued him and he became even more excited when he
learned that the owners of each were little pigs. He knocked on the door of
the straw house …

1. What other fairy tale is referred to during the story? (1 mark)

2. Why did the first little pig choose to build his house of straw? (2 marks)

3. Would you describe the third little pig as clever or foolish? Explain your answer fully using the text. (2 marks)

4. From your knowledge of fairy tales, write down the phrase that the wolf says when he knocks on the door of the house. (1 mark)

5. Why had the wolf not attacked them when they were building their houses? (1 mark)

6. Write down **two** features of this story (including your knowledge of the ending) that make it a fairy tale. (2 marks)

7. Mother pig could be described as having 'mixed emotions' about the little pigs leaving home. Why do you think she was both happy and sad about them leaving? (1 mark)

8. What does 'it seemed like the house grew smaller and smaller' mean? (1 mark)

9. What does the author want us to think about the character of the first little pig? Choose **one** option from the list below and explain your answer. (2 marks)

   brave   **clever**   **timid**   **unkind**

10. What is the name of the punctuation mark used at the end of the story? Choose **one** option from the list below and explain your answer. (2 marks)

   full stop   **speech mark**   **ellipsis**   **question mark**

11. Write the rest of the story, demonstrating your knowledge of this fairy tale. (3 marks)

Score ⬤ / 18

Play scripts

Play scripts are written versions of a play that are used by the actors in preparation for a performance.

The actors use the script during rehearsals so that they can practise the play. They need to think about how the characters are feeling and then say the lines with the right kind of emotion. By the final performance they must know the script by heart.

Who's Missing?

The scene is a classroom with the children sitting in groups around tables and the teacher standing at the front at her computer.

TEACHER   Shh! I am going to do the register now and I need to know who is missing as there are some empty spaces. Please don't speak whilst I do the register. Jamie …

Silence.

TEACHER   That's a good start. Jamie isn't here. I felt sure I had seen him this morning. Oh well, Megan …

Silence.

TEACHER   And Megan is away as well … This is not a good day. I hope they are not poorly. Mark …

Silence.

TEACHER   Oh dear, I hope that some people are here (*laughing and looking up from the register*). Phoebe …

Georgia *has her hand in the air and is making noises to attract* ***Teacher***.

TEACHER   What is it, Georgia? I told you not to interrupt during the register.

GEORGIA   Mrs Thomas, you didn't say don't interrupt. You said not to speak while you did the register … so nobody has.

TEACHER   (*sigh*) What is your point Georgia? Hurry up …

GEORGIA   Well, Jamie, Megan, Mark and Phoebe are all here but you told them not to speak so they didn't answer their names.

TEACHER   (*big sigh*) Oh dear, it is not going well this morning. Please, just tell me who is missing!

1 Work with a partner. Each read the words of a character in the play. Use the script to help you to act the play. Use the stage directions (the parts in italics) to help you to make it realistic. (1 mark)

2 From the list below, choose **one** word that best describes how the teacher is feeling. You may need to use a dictionary. (1 mark)

bored   **amused**   **furious**   **exasperated**

Test yourself

3 What is the name of the teacher? Choose **one** answer from the options below. (1 mark)

Mr James   **Miss Thomas**   **Thomas**   **Mrs Thomas**

4 Why did the children not answer when the teacher read out their names? (1 mark)

5 What instruction did the teacher mean to give to the children at the start of the register? (1 mark)

6 If the register is in alphabetical order by **surname**, write the names of the children in the order they were read out. (1 mark)

Jamie Day   **Megan Smith**   **Mark Brown**   **Phoebe Jones**

Challenge yourself

7 Rewrite the following line with a stage direction to show how the teacher is delivering the line. (1 mark)

TEACHER   What is it, Georgia? I told you not to interrupt during the register.

How did you do?

The structure of play scripts

A play script shows the **lines** (words) that need to be said next to each character's name.

It also shows **stage directions**, which give the actors information about how they should say their lines, how they should move and position themselves, where the scene is set, what scenery there is, and how any **props** (moveable stage items) should be used.

Who is the Best?

*The scene is a jungle clearing with a rock on which **Tiger** is standing at the beginning of the play. All the other animals are gathered around him.*

TIGER (*proudly*) I am the fiercest animal in this jungle and therefore I must be the best!

MONKEY (*a little bit scared*) Mr Tiger, are there not other things that are important?

TIGER (*laughing*) What could be more important than being fierce?

EAGLE (*flying up to the rock next to **Tiger***) What about being able to fly above the jungle and look for danger to warn others?

TIGER Pah! I don't need warning. I am the fiercest and the best!

***Eagle** flies off.*

ELEPHANT What about being the tallest and biggest animal in the jungle?

TIGER What use is that if you are not fiercer than me?

***Elephant** walks off shaking his head.*

CROCODILE What about having the biggest set of teeth and being able to hide in the water?

TIGER Um … your teeth are impressive, but you are still not as fierce as me.

***Crocodile** slithers off into the water.*

MONKEY (*still a little scared*) What about Mr Monkey being able to make a loud noise and swing through the trees?

TIGER What is the use of that, you silly monkey? Like I said, fiercest is the best!

***Monkey** swings off through the trees.*

SNAKE (*slithering along the ground*) What about being camouflaged so you can creep up on your prey? (*opens mouth and goes to attack the Tiger with a hissing sound*).

TIGER OK, OK! There are better things than being fierce. Please don't hurt me!

Warm up

1 How many characters have speaking parts in this scene? (1 mark)

2 What are the stage directions for in this scene? (2 marks)

Test yourself

3 Who thinks that being able to hide in the water is better than being the fiercest? Choose **one** option from the list below. (1 mark)

Monkey   **Crocodile**   **Eagle**   **Snake**

4 Why does Tiger change his mind about the fiercest being the best? (1 mark)

5 What strength does Eagle have that the others don't have? Why is this useful? (2 marks)

Challenge yourself

6 Do you think that any animal in the play is more important than the others? Explain your answer. (2 marks)

7 Rewrite the play script on page 18 into a short story. Use your own words to retell events, rather than copying from the text. You can use the words that the animals say but think carefully about your speech punctuation. (3 marks)

How did you do?

The language of poetry

Poems can be about almost anything. Poems can be very intense and sometimes they do not use very many words.

It is important to understand that while some poems **rhyme**, not all poems have to rhyme.

Rhythm is often very important in poetry.

Sometimes sentences can be broken up into separate lines on the page, and sometimes the lines can be grouped together in **stanzas**. Stanzas are normally separated by a line space.

On with the Show

Falling silently from leaden skies
with dancing, drifting clusters
of spiny webs,
winter takes a bow.

Beneath the crystal covering,
spring waits in the wings.
Chorus lines of snowdrops waiting
and it's on with the show.

Warm up

1. How many stanzas does this poem have? (1 mark)

2. Which of these statements about the poem is false? Choose **one** answer from the options below. (1 mark)

   - Sentences are broken up into separate lines.
   - It rhymes.
   - It uses just a few words to describe the scene.

3 What takes a bow? Choose **one** of the options from the list below. (1 mark)

winter   **autumn**   **summer**   **spring**

4 What is the word 'wings' referring to in this poem? Choose **one** of the options from the list below. (1 mark)

a bird's wings   **the wings at the edge of a stage**   **an aeroplane's wings**

5 What are there lines of? Choose **one** of the options from the list below. (1 mark)

snowdrops   **spiders' webs**   **puddles**   **snow**

6 One season is turning into another. Write the sentence out and fill in the blanks to show what is happening. (1 mark)

_____ is turning into _____ .

7 One of the lines says, 'Beneath the crystal covering'. To what is the poet referring? (1 mark)

8 The author has used **alliteration** (repetition of the same sound or letter at the start of a series of words) in the poem. Find **two** examples of this. (2 marks)

How did you do?

Identifying main ideas

The **main idea** of a text is not just the information from the beginning of the text or paragraph. Neither is it just what the text is about. The main idea is what the author wants the reader to understand as being important and valued within the text.

The first paragraph of a letter, for example, should introduce the main and most important idea. The following sentences and paragraphs should then add extra information to this idea.

> 14 Hazel Court
> Cossington
> CG4 0NE
>
> The Manager
> The Furniture Store
> High Street
> Cossington
> CG1 4BE
>
> 1st July
>
> Dear Sir/Madam,
>
> I am writing to complain about the table I bought from you last week, which was delivered to my house yesterday.
>
> Whilst the table itself is very smart and suitable for purpose, I do not think that you are thinking about the environment enough when you are running your company. The wood that the table is made from has, I believe, been cut down illegally in Thailand. Do you know that this, whilst keeping your profit high, is threatening the habitats of people and birds, let alone destroying the natural barrier against global warming? I am very worried about the environment but do not think you are.
>
> I feel strongly that you need to think more carefully about how your business is having a bad effect on the environment.
>
> Yours faithfully,
>
> Sam Smith

Pages 4–5
1. Any two fairy tales (**1 mark**)
2. Three from: talking animals, fairies, giants, elves, princes, princesses, kings, queens or other fairy tale character types (**1 mark**)
3. Three correct elements of fairy tales, e.g. storybook beginnings/endings, good characters, bad characters, royalty, magic (**1 mark**)
4. her parents (**1 mark**)
5. She was shocked/surprised to find that the frog was able to talk (**1 mark**)
6. She was hungry but she did not want to eat from the same plate as the frog because she was cross/unhappy/thought it was unhygienic (**2 marks** for answering that she was hungry but did not want to share the plate with the frog; **1 mark** for an answer that identifies she did not want to share the plate with the frog but does not link this with her being hungry)
7. He learned that it was better to be kind, polite and helpful rather than rude and demanding (**1 mark** for an answer that identifies that he learned that he should treat people well)
8. Any of: the fairy; the talking frog; the bewitching of the prince; the frog turning into a prince (**1 mark** for each correct feature stated; max. **2 marks**)
9. She was rude, ungrateful and unkind to people (**2 marks** for a complete answer, using evidence from text; **1 mark** for simply stating answer)

Pages 6–7
1. Opening: *Once upon a time*; Ending: *lived happily ever after* (**1 mark** for each)
2. Fairy Godmother; an old lady (**1 mark** for each)
3. Cinderella (**1 mark**)
4. **2 marks** for answering that they were angry with the mystery girl for dancing with the Prince and that they had wanted to dance with him/marry him; **1 mark** for an answer that identifies one of the above but does not link them
5. (1) Cinderella helped the Ugly Sisters get ready for the ball; (2) The Fairy Godmother transformed Cinderella; (3) Cinderella arrived at the ball; (4) The clock struck midnight; (5) Cinderella and the Prince got married (**2 marks** for all in correct order)
6. dazzling (**1 mark**)
7. Do not feel sorry for the Ugly Sisters as they had not been kind to Cinderella and had treated her like a slave, making her get their dresses ready for the ball. They did not help Cinderella find a dress or transport to the ball. They laughed at Cinderella when she tried on the slipper (**2 marks** for answer giving at least two reasons from list)

Pages 8–9
1. prince; princess; queen (maid also possible) (**1 mark** for each)
2. Fairy tales usually end with the good characters living happily ever after/getting married, like they do in this one (**1 mark**)
3. He couldn't find a real princess (**1 mark**)
4. Any one of the following: she did not have a maid/she was on her own/her clothes were dripping (**1 mark**)
5. lashed down (**1 mark**)
6. Because the princess could feel the pea under 25 mattresses and 25 quilts, which was a test and something only a princess would be sensitive enough to feel (**2 marks** for linking feeling the pea to this being a test for being a princess; **1 mark** for stating she felt the pea)
7. **2 marks** for identifying that the prince can only marry a princess because of tradition – it would not be right for him to marry an 'ordinary' girl; **1 mark** for identifying that the prince wanted to marry a princess

Pages 10–11
1. Peru (**1 mark**)
2. He thought it was a very long time – he worked out the number of hours it was going to be (**2 marks** for explaining how he felt with a reason; **1 mark** for just stating reason)
3. leaving messages (**1 mark**)
4. Because they had cancelled the milk, which meant he wouldn't have any while they were gone (**1 mark**)
5. 5 days (**1 mark**); because they have asked the milkman not to leave any milk for 5 days (**1 mark**)
6. No, because they have left him at home all by himself and gone to a different country without telling him. He is too young to be left at home alone as he is still at school and is 'about' 10 years old. They have cancelled all the milk (**2 marks** for an answer that gives at least two reasons; **1 mark** for only 1 reason)
7. It is in the bathroom, so they want him to remember to clean his teeth (**1 mark**)

Pages 12–13
1. The church bells are ringing; It is not Sunday (**1 mark** for both correct)
2. breakfast (**1 mark**)
3. The narrator knows what the ringing bells mean/'boats were wrecked on those rocks every year'/the narrator knows that the ship won't sink 'for now'/using the word 'always' when talking about rescuing the crew shows it has happened before/knowing that the boats will go out again after the crew are rescued (**2 marks** for any two)
4. She would not want the porridge wasted/she would want the narrator to have a good breakfast in the morning (**2 marks** for two; **1 mark** for only one)

Answers

5. His dad had put his boots on and rushed out of the house (**1 mark**); he must own a boat for the narrator to say 'Dad's boat' (**1 mark**)
6. The text says 'I knew the ship would not sink for now' (**1 mark**); 'There was always plenty of time to rescue the crew' (**1 mark**)
7. The final paragraph says that once the men from the ship were safely ashore, the boats would go back out again (**2 marks** for full answer; **1 mark** for stating that crew would be saved)
8. It will then sink, because the text says 'would not sink for now'. It has been damaged on the rocks and they are keeping it stuck while the tide is out. When the tide comes back in it will lift the boat off the rocks and then it will sink because of the holes in it (**2 marks** for full answer; **1 mark** for answer that says it will sink but without explanation)

Pages 14–15
1. Little Red Riding Hood (**1 mark**)
2. It was quick to build (**1 mark**); he was scared of the dark and wanted to build it quickly (**1 mark**)
3. Clever (**1 mark**); because he took his time to plan his house so it was sturdy and safe (**1 mark**)
4. 'Little Pig, Little Pig, let me come in!' (**1 mark**)
5. He had been away on holiday in a different wood and had been busy terrorising a girl in a red cloak (**1 mark**)
6. Story language/talking animals/bad character defeated in the end/good characters live happily ever after (**2 marks** for two or more; **1 mark** for only one)
7. She would miss them/they had lived there since they were small/she would be lonely (**1 mark**)
8. The house could not actually shrink but as the pigs grew bigger, there was less space so it appeared that the house was smaller (**1 mark**)
9. timid (**1 mark**); he was scared of the dark (**1 mark**)
10. ellipsis (**1 mark**); it means that the story continues (**1 mark**)
11. **3 marks** for complete ending

Pages 16–17
1. **1 mark** for correct reading
2. exasperated (**1 mark**)
3. Mrs Thomas (**1 mark**)
4. She had told them not to speak whilst she did the register (**1 mark**)
5. Not to speak unless answering their names (**1 mark**)
6. Mark Brown, Jamie Day, Phoebe Jones, Megan Smith (**1 mark**)
7. exasperated/crossly/irritable (or similar) (**1 mark**)

Pages 18–19
1. six (**1 mark**)
2. To give the actors information about how they should say their lines/move/position themselves/what scenery there is (**1 mark** for each; max. **2 marks**)
3. Crocodile (**1 mark**)
4. The snake is about to attack him (**1 mark**)
5. He can fly (**1 mark**); he can check for danger in the forest below (**1 mark**)
6. No (**1 mark**); because each animal has different strengths and weaknesses and therefore you cannot compare them with each other (**1 mark**)
7. Max. **3 marks**

Pages 20–21
1. two (**1 mark**)
2. It rhymes (**1 mark**)
3. winter (**1 mark**)
4. the wings at the edge of a stage (**1 mark**)
5. snowdrops (**1 mark**)
6. Winter is turning into spring (**1 mark** for the seasons written in the correct order)
7. Snow/ice/frost covering surface of ground (**1 mark**)
8. dancing, drifting/crystal covering (**1 mark** for each)

Pages 22–23
1. He doesn't think the manager cares about the environment (**2 marks**)
2. Illegal logging in Thailand/the threat to the habitats of people and birds/the destruction of the natural barrier against global warming (**2 marks** for two or three; **1 mark** for one)
3. The Furniture Store (**1 mark**)
4. Sam's (**1 mark**)
5. Example answers: Do you want to keep the table?; Where did you get your information from?; If you are worried about the environment, why did you buy the table? (**1 mark** for a question that refers to Sam's complaint and action)
6. **No**; he likes his table/he chose to buy from that shop knowing their policy/there is nothing wrong with the table. Accept **yes**; as long as a valid argument is given. (**2 marks** for 2 plausible reasons)
7. Yours sincerely (**1 mark**)

Pages 24–25
1. Where: penguin enclosure at the zoo; When: 12.15 pm on Saturday; Why witness was there: waiting to watch penguins feed (**1 mark** for each)
2. Example answer: A girl dropped her camera into the penguin enclosure. Her dad was cross. He lifted her over the wall. She wanted to get nearer to the penguins. Her dad shouted because he thought they were attacking her. The keeper lifted her and the camera out (**2 marks** for correct answer of 50 or fewer words; **1 mark** for a summary a little over 50 words)

Answers

3. her dad (**1 mark**)
4. No, because she wanted to get nearer to them and she did not run away or cry when they approached her (**2 marks** for stating No with explanation from text; **1 mark** for stating No but with an explanation not based on text)
5. No (**1 mark**); the penguins were friendly and one of them nuzzled her hand (**1 mark**)
6. It was time for the keepers to feed the penguins and they learn where the food comes into the enclosure so they were waiting on the rock for it (**1 mark**)
7. Cross, because: the signs told people not to enter the penguin enclosure/the girl approached the penguins herself/the penguins weren't hurting the girl/the man was shouting at him (**2 marks** for two or more; **1 mark** for only one)

Pages 26–27
1. Email (**1 mark**); because of the address at the top of the page, the icons and the layout features (**1 mark** for one of these)
2. **3 marks** for correct answer in email format
3. Australia (**1 mark**)
4. Rebecca (**1 mark**)
5. No, because Freya asks her about her new house and school, which means she is living there, not just there on holiday (**2 marks** for identifying 'No' and giving reasons based on evidence from the text; **1 mark** for identifying 'No' but reason not based on textual evidence)
6. Yes – 'which is keeping me busy and is annoying' (**2 marks** for Yes and quoting line from text; **1 mark** for Yes but not using quotation from text)
7. Example answers: Hi/How are you doing?/use of contractions like 'isn't'/BTW/loads and loads of hugs (**2 marks** for two or three correct, **1 mark** for one)

Pages 28–29
1. They rhyme (**1 mark**)
2. Grandma is small and tough (**1 mark**)
3. coat, hat, shoes (**2 marks** for all three; **1 mark** for two)
4. Yes (**1 mark**); He thought that grandma was 'tough' and says that she will be like 'caviar' (something that is considered very tasty) (**1 mark**)
5. He is made into a wolfskin coat for Little Red Riding Hood (**1 mark**)
6. He tells Red Riding Hood that she has forgotten to ask about his teeth (**1 mark**)
7. **LRRH**   What great big ears you have, Grandma.
   Wolf   All the better to hear you with.
   LRRH   What great big eyes you have, Grandma.
   Wolf   All the better to see you with. (**2 marks**)
8. The woodcutter (**1 mark**)
9. helping (**1 mark**)

10. Summaries should tell the whole story but in only 50 words (**2 marks** for correct summaries of 50 words; **1 mark** for correct summaries just over 50 words)

Pages 30–31
1. The **author** has used **sub-headings** to help structure this **explanation** text and help the **reader** to understand it in more detail. (**2 marks** for all correct; **1 mark** for two or three)
2. The diagram shows the water cycle and how water rises and falls, which is what the paragraph is describing (**1 mark**)
3. water vapour (**1 mark**)
4. hydropower (**1 mark**)
5. Water (**1 mark**); as the text says that electricity can be created by water (**1 mark**)
6. It has labelled diagrams/no headline/no quotes from people/it has bullet points (**2 marks** for two or more; **1 mark** for one)
7. **3 marks**; 1 for each correctly written fact

Pages 32–33
1. Diary (**1 mark**); because it says 'Dear Diary' at the beginning (**1 mark**)
2. wicked/mum/dad/granny/grandpa/best bit/Daddy/didn't/well/cool/thing/stuff/cos/fab/loads/I'm/gonna/gotta/tho/boo (**2 marks** for three correct examples; **1 mark** for two)
3. Grandpa (**1 mark**)
4. inflatable boat (**1 mark**)
5. Daddy pulled a fast boat/Granny wins on 2p machines/Matilda owns a 'cool bucket thing' (**2 marks** for all three correct; **1 mark** for two)
6. No (**1 mark**); it says 'Boo' at the end of the diary (**1 mark**)
7. Example answer: My cousin had a bucket which made little sandcastles and which allowed you to stick arms, eyes, ears and other funny features on it (just like Mr Potato Head). I was quite jealous because it was great fun, but Matilda let me share it, so I got to play with it a lot too (**2 marks** for a paragraph that contains the same information in a formal tone; **1 mark** for a paragraph that has mostly formal but some informal words/tone)
8. Check that pupils are using an informal tone in their writing (**3 marks** for a full informal entry)

Pages 34–35
1. Any three of the following: to retell an event or series of events; to tell someone how to make or do something; to discuss an issue or offer two or more points of view; to give an account of how or why something happens (**2 marks** for three correct; **1 mark** for one or two correct)
2. Example answers: recipes, rules, directions (**1 mark** for each correct answer to max. **2 marks**)

Answers

3. recount (**1 mark**)
4. Details of a friction experiment is a recount text. A traveller's guide to Australia is a discussion text. Why does rain fall? is an explanation text (**2 marks** for all three correct; **1 mark** for one or two)
5. Example answer: explanation of the water cycle; explanation of why fish have gills (**1 mark** for each suitable answer to max. **2 marks**)
6. If the audience is small children, you need to use simple language, pictures and write about things they understand (**2 marks** for full answer; **1 mark** for a shorter answer)
7. leaflets/adverts/debate texts/persuasive letters/posters (**2 marks** for two correct examples; **1 mark** for one)

Pages 36–37
1. alphabetically (**1 mark**)
2. Example answer: What equipment do you need? (Accept any question beginning with a capital letter and finishing with a question mark that would be relevant for the rowing section; **2 marks**)
3. 23 (**1 mark**)
4. diving (**1 mark**)
5. 5–11 year olds (**1 mark**); because it mentions 'school sports' (**1 mark**)
6. A glossary gives definitions of the technical words in the book (**2 marks** for explanation that states definitions of technical words/vocabulary; **1 mark** that only states definitions of words/vocabulary)
7. Index has a list of topics from the book in alphabetical order; contents page gives topic title for each set of pages (**1 mark**)
8. **2 marks** for all correct; **1 mark** for one or two correctly written facts

Pages 38–39
1. bold headings, colour, questions, different sized text, illustration (**1 mark**)
2. when it is; where it is; what it is (**2 marks** for three correct; **1 mark** for one or two correct)
3. 6 (**1 mark**)
4. summer (**1 mark**)
5. Example answers: Details of more events/cost of activities/age restrictions (**1 mark** for each relevant idea up to a total of **2 marks**; the information should be additional to the poster's content)
6. Yes or No possible; pupils should explain their answer with reference to a feature from the text to gain **1 mark**
7. **1 mark** for each correctly labelled sign up to max. **3 marks**
8. The writer went to the seaside with their family/they went in a boat/they built a sandcastle/they went to the amusements/they enjoyed it (**2 marks** for key

information only; **1 mark** for key information but a small amount of additional information)

Pages 40–41
1. **What?** wildlife park; **Where?** heart of England; **Where can you have a hot meal?** Tiger Tavern; **How can you save £2 per person?** book online; **Name four living animals you will see:** Any four from: lions, monkeys, wolves, crocodiles, camels and white tigers (3 marks for all correct; **2 marks** for three or four correct; **1 mark** for two correct)
2. Example answers: photos, illustrations, bright colours, park map. (**1 mark** for at least three examples)
3. High-Wire Tree Adventure (**1 mark**)
4. fast food (**1 mark**)
5. fantastic/fun/huge/numerous/exciting/brilliant/excellent (**1 mark** for each correct word, max. **2 marks**)
6. **2 marks** for statement and explanation; **1 mark** for just statement with a non-detailed explanation
7. **1 mark** for each correct similarity; max. **3 marks**

Pages 42–43
1. instructions (**1 mark**); features: materials list/numbered steps/imperative verbs (**1 mark** for one feature)
2. children (**1 mark**); children build dens/it says ask for adult help/babies would not be able to read instructions (**1 mark** for one reason)
3. Excited; they say 'have fun' at the end (**1 mark**)
4. Because they are being used in a den and they don't want sheets to be taken off beds (**1 mark**)
5. Sofas are heavy and the instructions are written for children so they would be too heavy to move on their own (**1 mark**)
6. e.g. circus tent/woodland den/hospital ward (**2 marks** for three plausible examples; **1 mark** for two plausible examples)
7. e.g. How do I stand the cushions up?/How many cushions do I need to use for the doors? (**1 mark** for correctly punctuated, plausible question)
8. Not a story/written in numbered steps/no paragraphs (**2 marks**; 1 for each correct difference)
9. lights/white sheets/white blankets/snowflake decorations (**1 mark** for each plausible suggestion; max. **2 marks**)
10. You can imagine that the den is anything/anywhere you want it to be. Your imagination can take it away from being a den in your living room to being a palace in Egypt (for example) (**1 mark** for a clear explanation of the phrase)
11. A clear set of instructions written using the same style and features as required (max. **3 marks**)

1 Why is Sam cross? Choose **one** of the options from the list below. (2 marks)

- He doesn't like the look of the table.
- His delivery was late.
- He had bad service at the store.
- He doesn't think the manager cares about the environment.

2 What, in particular, is Sam concerned about? (2 marks)

3 What is the name of the shop that Sam has written to? Choose **one** of the options from the list below. (1 mark)

The Furniture Store   **14 Hazel Court**   **Cossington**   **The High Street**

4 Whose address is in the top right-hand corner? Choose **one** of the options from the list below. (1 mark)

the manager's   **Sam's**   **the shop's**   **the table's**

5 If you were the manager, what question might you ask Sam in response? (1 mark)

6 Do you think that Sam is correct to complain to the manager about his issue? (2 marks)

7 If Sam had written to the manager of the shop by name (for example, Mr Boyd), how would he need to end his letter to ensure that it is formal? (1 mark)

How did you do?

Summarising ideas

It is important to be able to **summarise** information from one or a number of sources, so you can draw out the key points without re-reading everything.

After an accident or crime, for example, the police sometimes have to collect and study statements from the people who saw it happen (the witnesses). If you had 20 witness statements about one event, you could pull out the points that were consistent between them and create a summary of what occurred, based on the different accounts.

Witness Statement

I was standing by the penguin enclosure at the zoo at about 12.15pm on Saturday. There were people standing all around the walls, as we were waiting for the keepers to come and feed the penguins. I was watching the penguins, which were huddled together on what I believe must be their feeding rock.

Suddenly, my attention was drawn to the other end of the enclosure where a man was shouting at a little girl. He said, 'I told you to hold on to it carefully!' The little girl (who was around nine years old) was crying. It was then that I noticed a camera just below them, in the penguin enclosure.

The man then lifted the little girl up over the small wall and let her down into the penguin enclosure. Lots of people gasped as the signs clearly said, 'Do not enter the penguin enclosure.' The little girl was no longer crying. Instead of getting the camera, she walked closer to the penguins, which all began to move towards her. She put out her hand to touch one and it nuzzled her hand.

It was at this moment that her dad yelled, 'Help! Help! The penguins are attacking my daughter!' The keepers arrived for the feeding and he immediately began shouting at them. One of the keepers dropped into the enclosure, picked up the girl (and the camera) and handed both back to the shouting man.

1 Write **three** bullets points to list the key information from the first paragraph. Use the headings below to help you. (3 marks)

- Where

- When

- Why witness was there

2 Write a summary of what happened in no more than **50** words. (2 marks)

Test yourself

3 What relation was the man to the girl? Choose **one** of the options from the list below. (1 mark)

her brother   **the zoo keeper**   **her dad**   **her uncle**

4 Was the girl scared of the penguins? How do you know? (2 marks)

5 Were the penguins attacking the little girl? Explain your answer. (2 marks)

Challenge yourself

6 Why do you think the author deduced that the penguins were huddled on their 'feeding rock'? (1 mark)

7 How do you think the keeper felt towards the man and the little girl? Explain your reasons using evidence from the text. (2 marks)

How did you do?

Presentation and meaning

The way that text is **presented** can signal lots of information to the reader. For example, if you glance at a piece of paper and see an address in the top right-hand corner, you know this is likely to be a letter. Similarly, if you see a text with a big headline and columns of writing underneath it, you think 'newspaper'.

Presentation can play a key role in how a reader understands a text. You therefore need to be familiar with the standard layout features of different text types.

1 What type of text is this? How do you know? (2 marks)

2 Write a reply to Freya (in the role of Maddy) in the same style. Make sure that you answer the questions that Freya asks. (3 marks)

3 Where is Maddy now? Choose **one** of the options from the list below. (1 mark)

England   **America**   **Ireland**   **Australia**

4 Who had an argument with Abbie? Choose **one** of the options from the list below. (1 mark)

Freya   **Rebecca**   **Maddy**   **Vicky**

5 Maddy has gone on holiday. Is this correct? Explain your answer. (2 marks)

6 Has Freya agreed to pass messages between the two girls who are arguing? Which words tell you this? (2 marks)

7 Some informal words and phrases are used in this text that would not be used in a formal letter. Write **three** examples of this. (2 marks)

How did you do?

Little Red Riding Hood and the Wolf, by Roald Dahl

I

As soon as Wolf began to feel
That he would like a decent meal,
He went and knocked on Grandma's door.
When Grandma opened it, she saw
The sharp white teeth, the horrid grin,
And Wolfie said, 'May I come in?'
Poor Grandmamma was terrified,
'He's going to eat me up!' she cried.
And she was absolutely right.
He ate her up in one big bite.
But Grandmamma was small and tough,
And Wolfie wailed, 'That's not enough!
'I haven't yet begun to feel
That I have had a decent meal!'
He ran around the kitchen yelping,
'I've *got* to have another helping!'
Then added with a frightful leer,
'I'm therefore going to wait right here
'Till Little Miss Red Riding Hood
Comes home from walking in the wood.'
He quickly put on Grandma's clothes,
(Of course he hadn't eaten those.)
He dressed himself in coat and hat.
He put on shoes, and after that
He even brushed and curled his hair,
Then sat himself in Grandma's chair.
In came the little girl in red.
She stopped. She stared. And then she said,

II

'What great big ears you have, Grandma.'
'All the better to hear you with,' the Wolf replied.
'What great big eyes you have, Grandma,' said Little Red Riding Hood.
'All the better to see you with,' the Wolf replied.

III

He sat there watching her and smiled.
He thought, I'm going to eat this child.
Compared with her old Grandmamma
She's going to taste like caviar.

IV

Then Little Red Riding Hood said,
'But Grandma, what a lovely great big furry coat you have on.'

V

'That's wrong!' cried Wolf. 'Have you forgot
To tell me what BIG TEETH I've got?
Ah well, no matter what you say,
I'm going to eat you anyway.'
The small girl smiles. One eyelid flickers.
She whips a pistol from her knickers.
She aims it at the creature's head
And *bang bang bang*, she shoots him dead.
A few weeks later, in the wood,
I came across Miss Riding Hood.
But what a change! No cloak of red,
No silly hood upon her head.
She said, 'Hello, and do please note
My lovely furry wolfskin coat.'

1 What do you notice about the end of each pair of lines in the poem?   (1 mark)

2 Why does the wolf complain that he has not had a decent meal?   (1 mark)

3 What was the wolf wearing when Little Red Riding Hood arrived?   (2 marks)

4 Does the wolf think that Little Red Riding Hood will taste better than her grandma? Explain using the text.   (2 marks)

5 What happens to the wolf after Red Riding Hood kills him?   (1 mark)

6 How do you know that the wolf already knows the story of Little Red Riding Hood? Choose **one** answer from the options below.   (1 mark)

  • He tells Red Riding Hood that she is tasty.

  • He tells Red Riding Hood that she has forgotten to ask about his teeth.

  • He tells Red Riding Hood that her granny is dead.

7 Rewrite stanza **II** into a play script. Remember to use all the features of a play script.   (2 marks)

8 Which character is missing from this poem that is in the traditional fairy tale?   (1 mark)

9 Find and copy the word that is used to rhyme with 'yelping'.   (1 mark)

10 Write a short summary of the main points of the story in no more than **50** words.   (2 marks)

Score ⬭ /14

Structure and meaning

Text **structure** refers to the way that an author organises the text. The way the text is set out depends on the type of text it is and what it is for.

For example, a formal letter will be arranged based on the usual way that this type of text is written, whilst an explanation text will be laid out to help the reader understand and remember information, perhaps using headings, sub-headings, diagrams and bullet points.

Rain

How does rain form?

Water droplets are formed when warm air (which holds lots of water) rises into the sky and then cools. Water vapour is always in the air – we just can't see it! When enough of the water droplets collect together, they form a cloud. If the clouds grow in size and contain enough water droplets, the droplets knock together and form even bigger drops. When the drops become too heavy, they fall (due to gravity) as rain.

More rain facts:

- Water can also fall from the sky as hail, sleet or snow.

- If rain is particularly heavy, it can cause flooding and landslides.

- We can create electricity using water. This is called **hydropower**.

DID YOU KNOW?

The highest amount of rainfall ever recorded in one year is 25.4 m, in Cherrapunji, India.

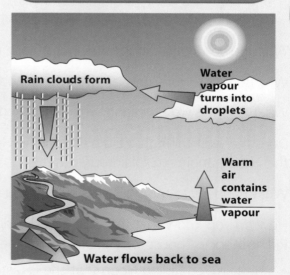

Rain clouds form

Water vapour turns into droplets

Warm air contains water vapour

Water flows back to sea

Rain is a key part of the water cycle.

1 Use the words in the box to fill in the spaces in the sentence below. (2 marks)

> author   reader   explanation   sub-headings

The _____ has used _____ to help structure this _____ text and help the _____ to understand it in more detail.

2 How does the diagram help the reader understand the information in the first paragraph better? (1 mark)

Test yourself

3 What is in the air but cannot be seen? Choose **one** of the options from the list below. (1 mark)

rain   **snow**   **water vapour**   **hail**

4 What is electricity created by water called? Choose **one** of the options from the list below. (1 mark)

hydropower   **hyperpower**   **waterpower**   **rainpower**

5 What do you think *hydro* might mean in the term 'hydropower'? Explain your answer. (2 marks)

Challenge yourself

6 Explain, giving examples from the text, how this explanation text differs in structure to a newspaper report. (2 marks)

7 Read another explanation text about rain from a book in your school. Write down **three** facts that you learn from this text. (3 marks)

How did you do?

Language and meaning

The people that the text is aimed at, and what the text is for, will decide the type of **language** that is used in text.

For example, if the text is a letter to your teacher, you would use **formal** language.

In contrast, a diary entry might include **informal** language, slang terms and abbreviations.

Dear Diary,

What a wicked day! I went to the beach with my mum, dad, granny, grandpa, uncle, auntie and little cousin. It was so hot that we were able to stay there all day! Grandpa made an amazing sandcastle that was enormous. He even made a ramp so that a ball rolled down from the top to the moat!

My best bit was going in the inflatable boat and being pulled in fast by Daddy so that it felt like a speedboat. Water even came up over the front and into the boat!!

I also loved it when we went to the amusements, even though we didn't win anything! We never do. Well, sometimes Granny wins on the 2p machines, but I never have!

My cousin had this cool bucket thing where you made a little sandcastle using the bucket and then stuck on arms, eyes, ears and other funny stuff (just like my Mr Potato Head). I was quite jealous cos it was fab, but Matilda let me share it, so I still got to play with it loads.

I also collected lots of shells that I'm gonna clean tomorrow, so I can make a pattern with them for my bedroom wall…

Gotta get some sleep now tho cos I've got to go to school tomorrow. Boo!

1 What type of text is this? How do you know? (2 marks)

2 Some informal words are used in this text that would not be used in formal text. Find **three** examples of these words. (2 marks)

3 Who made an 'amazing sandcastle'? Choose **one** of the options from the list below. (1 mark)

Matilda   **Daddy**   **Grandpa**   **Granny**

4 What was the author's best bit? Choose **one** of the options from the list below. (1 mark)

sandcastles   **inflatable boat**   **amusements**   **shells**

5 Match the person to the action or description that refers to them. (2 marks)

wins on 2p machines	Daddy
owns a 'cool bucket thing'	Granny
pulled a fast boat	Matilda

6 Is the author looking forward to going back to school? How do you know? (2 marks)

7 Rewrite the fourth paragraph to make it sound formal. (2 marks)

8 Write a short diary entry in an informal way (like the one on page 32) about a day that you have enjoyed. (3 marks)

How did you do?

Types of non-fiction text

Non-fiction is a type of writing based on real-life events or facts, as opposed to a made-up story (fiction).

There are lots of different forms of non-fiction. When you have identified the text type, you need to think about the audience (who the text is aimed at) and the purpose (what the text is trying to do).

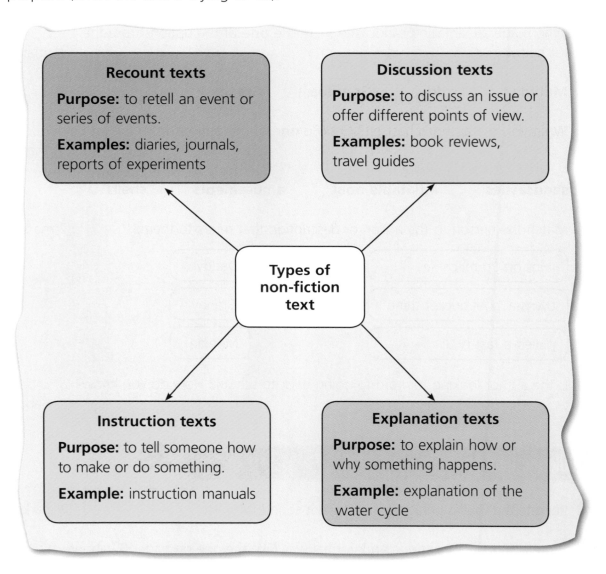

Recount texts

Purpose: to retell an event or series of events.

Examples: diaries, journals, reports of experiments

Discussion texts

Purpose: to discuss an issue or offer different points of view.

Examples: book reviews, travel guides

Types of non-fiction text

Instruction texts

Purpose: to tell someone how to make or do something.

Example: instruction manuals

Explanation texts

Purpose: to explain how or why something happens.

Example: explanation of the water cycle

1 Write **three** different purposes that non-fiction texts can have. (2 marks)

2 Write **two** more examples that could go in the 'instruction texts' box (two other types of text that are instructional). (2 marks)

Test yourself

3 What type of text is a diary? Choose **one** answer from the options below. (1 mark)

recount　　　**discussion**　　　**explanation**　　　**persuasion**

4 Match the type of text to the correct example. Then write sentences to show your answers. (2 marks)

discussion text	details of a friction experiment
explanation text	A traveller's guide to Australia
recount text	Why does rain fall?

5 Suggest **two** other topics that might be covered in an explanation text. (2 marks)

Challenge yourself

6 If you were writing an explanation text for young children, what would you need to think about? (2 marks)

7 A persuasive text is written to try to convince others of your point of view. Give **two** examples of persuasive texts you have read. (2 marks)

How did you do?

Asking questions

When reading, it is important to **ask questions** about the text to ensure that you are fully engaged with it. You need to think about what the author wants the reader to understand. As the reader, you need to ask questions, such as:

- Why has the author chosen to write in this way?
- Who is the text aimed at?
- How is it organised?

Contents

1 In what order are the sports listed in this book? (1 mark)

2 Write a question that could be answered in the pages about rowing. (1 mark)

3 To which page should you turn to learn about a game that uses a net, rackets and a small, yellow ball? Choose **one** answer from the options below. (1 mark)

21   **19**   **25**   **23**

4 What can you learn about on page 9? Choose **one** of the options from the list below. (1 mark)

diving   **swimming**   **archery**   **basketball**

5 Which group of people do you think the book is for? Choose **one** of the options from the list below. Explain your answer. (2 marks)

0–4 year olds   **5–11 year olds**   **Adults**

6 What is a glossary (page 32) for? (2 marks)

7 How does an index differ from a contents page? (1 mark)

8 Find a book about sport in your class book corner, school library or local library. Choose one of the sports from the contents page on page 36 and read about it. Write **three** questions about your chosen sport. (2 marks)

How did you do?

Retrieving information 1

To be a good reader you need to be able to skim read (look quickly through the text without reading every part) to identify the key information.

This is what advertising and public notices such as posters, road signs and flyers rely upon. They are designed to be read quickly (maybe from a car) and need to get the information across to the reader quickly.

You need to be able to skim the text and understand the information at speed.

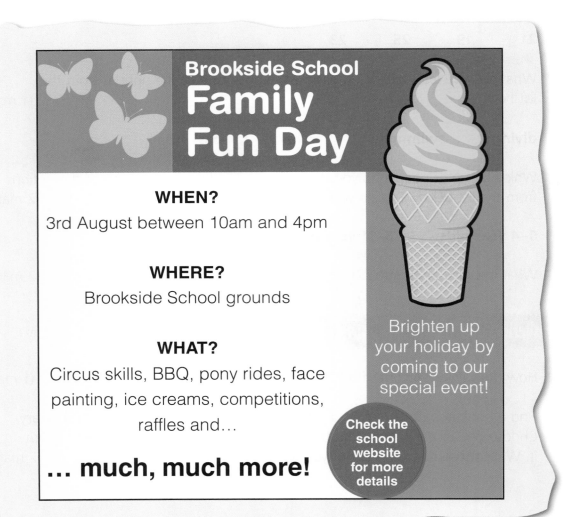

Brookside School
Family Fun Day

WHEN?
3rd August between 10am and 4pm

WHERE?
Brookside School grounds

WHAT?
Circus skills, BBQ, pony rides, face painting, ice creams, competitions, raffles and…

… much, much more!

Brighten up your holiday by coming to our special event!

Check the school website for more details

1 How does the text make the main information stand out? (1 mark)

2 What **three** main pieces of information does the poster give? (2 marks)

Test yourself

3 How many hours does the event last? Choose **one** of the options from the list below. (1 mark)

4   **5**   **6**   **10**

4 What time of year does the event take place in? Choose **one** answer from the options below. (1 mark)

autumn   **summer**   **spring**   **winter**

5 What other information might be on the website that is not on the poster? (2 marks)

6 Do you think this poster is good for giving information? Explain your answer. (1 mark)

Challenge yourself

7 Draw and label **three** signs that you might see around your school, which are designed to be read and understood quickly, for example, no entry, direction signs, classroom labels. (3 marks)

8 Re-read the text on page 32. Identify **five** key pieces of information you learn from the text that would summarise the day. (2 marks)

How did you do?

Retrieving information 2

The way in which information is provided depends on the purpose and the audience. The author needs to think about how long the reader has to take in the information. For example, an advert by the side of the road has to communicate information quickly to people passing by, whereas a leaflet (which can be picked up and taken away) can give more detailed information, although it still needs to be eye-catching.

WHAT IS BOWLER'S?

Bowler's Wildlife Park offers a fantastic, fun day out in the heart of England. There is so much to ZOO! We have a huge range of animals, including lions, monkeys, wolves, crocodiles, camels and even WHITE TIGERS! As well as the animals, we have an Indoor Playbarn, Woodland Railway, Safari Ride, Dinosaur Kingdom and – NEW FOR THIS YEAR – a High-Wire Tree Adventure!

FOOD AND DRINK

Bowler's has a huge selection of places to eat and drink: Tiger Tavern offers a range of hot and cold meals for the whole family; Crocodile Creek provides snacks and fast food; and numerous stalls around the park offer drinks, ice cream and other exciting treats. In fact, EVERYTHING you need for a brilliant day out is here!

HOW DO WE GET TO BOWLER'S?

Bowler's is situated just off the M5 at Junction 2. Use the postcode DY2 5HG if using a satnav. There is a bus station 2 minutes' walk from the wildlife park entrance. It has excellent rail routes – check the rail network's website for details.

BOOK ONLINE AND SAVE £2 PER PERSON.

1 Summarise the key information from the leaflet by answering the following questions. (3 marks)

- What is Bowler's?
- Where is it?
- Where can you have a hot meal?
- How can you save £2 per person?
- Name four living animals you will see.

2 This extract shows only the words from the leaflet. What else might the leaflet include? (1 mark)

3 What is new for this year? Choose **one** option from the list below. (1 mark)

High-Wire Tree Adventure   **Dinosaur Kingdom**

Woodland Railway   **white tigers**

4 What does the leaflet say that Crocodile Creek offers? Choose **one** option from the list below. (1 mark)

crocodiles   **fast food**   **ice cream**   **fun**

5 Write down **two** different adjectives that are used to make the park sound appealing. (2 marks)

6 Which of the things at Bowler's would you most like to see? Explain your answer. (2 marks)

7 Find a leaflet for a different animal park, either online or in paper format. Look carefully at it and identify **three** similarities between the text of the leaflet about Bowler's on page 40 and the one you have chosen. (3 marks)

How did you do?

How to build a den at home

Materials

Sofas

Old sheets

Clothes pegs

Blankets

Imagination!

Permission from an adult

Steps

1. Seek permission (and help) from an adult to move the furniture.

2. Choose what your den is going to be, e.g. a fairytale castle, a medieval castle, an underwater kingdom, an ice palace …

3. Move the sofas so that their backs are opposite each other, leaving the gap between that will be the part of the den that you enter.

4. Use large sheets and drape them over the top of the hole you have created, tucking them down between the back of the sofa and the cushions. Use as many as you like, depending on how dark you want your den to be inside. Use clothes pegs to secure the blankets to one another if required.

5. Use seat cushions from the sofas to create a door at the front of your den that can be swung open or closed to get in and out.

6. Use the blankets inside your den to make it comfortable or to be the floor of your chosen den.

7. Use your imagination to add decorations for the theme you have chosen – perhaps make snowflakes for an ice palace or crepe paper seaweed for an underwater kingdom.

8. Have fun playing in your creation and let your imagination take you to distant worlds.

1 What type of text is this? Choose **one** option from the list below and explain your answer by listing the features of that text type. (2 marks)

    recount   **instructions**   **explanation**   **discussion**

2 Who is the audience for this text? Choose **one** option from the list below and explain your answer fully. (1 mark)

    adults   **babies**   **children**   **teachers**

3 How does the author want the reader to feel about making dens? Explain your answer using evidence from the text. (1 mark)

4 Why does the author say to use 'old sheets'? (1 mark)

5 Why might you need 'help from an adult' to move the furniture? (1 mark)

6 Write a list of **three** other types of den that you could build. (2 marks)

7 Write a question to the author, to find out more details about how to create the 'doors' for the den. (1 mark)

8 Give **two** ways that this text is different from a fiction text. (2 marks)

9 Suggest **two** additional ways in which you could add decorations to create an 'ice palace'. (2 marks)

10 Explain what the author means when she says 'let your imagination take you to distant worlds'. (1 mark)

11 Choose a playground game that you play with your friends. Write a non-fiction text, like the one on page 42, to explain to somebody new how to play the game. (3 marks)

Acknowledgements

The author and publisher are grateful to the copyright holders for permission to use quoted materials and images.

Page 10 from *Grimble* by Clement Freud, reproduced with the kind permission of the Estate of Clement Freud.

Page 12 'Shipwreck' and page 20 'On with the Show', reproduced with the kind permission of Alison Head.

Page 28 'Little Red Riding Hood and the Wolf' from *Revolting Rhymes* by Roald Dahl, published by Jonathan Cape Ltd & Penguin Books Ltd; reproduced with the kind permission of David Higham Associates Limited, and in the USA by permission of Random House LLC.

Every effort has been made to trace copyright holders and obtain their permission for the use of copyright material. The author and publisher will gladly receive information enabling them to rectify any error or omission in subsequent editions. All facts are correct at the time of going to press.

Published by Keen Kite Books
An imprint of HarperCollins*Publishers* Ltd
1 London Bridge Street
London SE1 9GF

ISBN 9780008161705

First published in 2015

10 9 8 7 6 5 4 3 2

Text and design © 2015 Keen Kite Books, an imprint of HarperCollins*Publishers* Ltd

Author: Rachel Axten-Higgs

Series Concept and Commissioning: Michelle I'Anson
Series Editor and Development: Shelley Teasdale
Inside Concept Design: Paul Oates
Project Manager: Jane Moody
Cover Design: Carolyn Gibson
Text Design and Layout: Q2A Media
Production: Niccolò de Bianchi
Printed and bound by RR Donnelley APS

A CIP record of this book is available from the British Library.

Images are ©Shutterstock.com